STAR WARS®

JEDI ACADEMY

LEVIATHAN

STAR WARS®
JEDI ACADEMY
LEVIATHAN

story
KEVIN J. ANDERSON

pencils
DARIO CARRASCO, JR.

inks
MARK HEIKE with BILL BLACK
and DAVID JACOB BECKETT

color design
RAY MURTAUGH

color rendering
HAROLD MACKINNON

lettering
STEVE DUTRO

cover art
DAVID MICHAEL BECK

DARK HORSE COMICS®

publisher
MIKE RICHARDSON

series editor
DAVID LAND

collection editor
CHRIS WARNER

collection designer
JEREMY PERKINS

art director
MARK COX

Special thanks to **Allan Kausch** and **Lucy Autrey Wilson** at **Lucas Licensing**.

STAR WARS®: JEDI ACADEMY — LEVIATHAN

This book collects issues one through four of the Dark Horse comic-book series *Star Wars®: Jedi Academy – Leviathan.*

Published by
Dark Horse Comics, Inc.
10956 SE Main Street
Milwaukie, OR 97222

www.darkhorse.com

To find a comics shop in your area, call the Comic Shop Locator Service toll free at 1-888-266-4226

First edition: July 2000
ISBN: 1-56971-456-8

1 3 5 7 9 10 8 6 4 2

Printed in Canada

Vith the dawn of a New Republic, ıfter years of the Empire's larkness, new protectors arise — Jedi Knights, heroes who ıave served the Force for a housand generations.
Now, eight years since the all of the Emperor and the leath of Darth Vader, Luke kywalker begins to ee the results of his efforts to seek ɔut those with the ɔotential to use the Force.
n the ruins of an old ɔase, which was at one ɔne time nearly lestroyed by the irst Death Star, Luke has trained ıis candidates.
The first of them ıave learned to ɔe Jedi, and they must now begin their great work for the good of the galaxy.
THE FORCE IS EVERYWHERE.
BUT STUDENTS COME HERE, TO YAVIN FOUR, TO LEARN THE WAYS OF THE JEDI.
SOON THE JEDI KNIGHTS WILL RETURN, LIKE THE HEROES OF THE PAST.
THEY WILL BE PROTECTORS OF THE NEW REPUBLIC, JUST LIKE THE ONES IN THE STORIES OBI-WAN TOLD ME.

MY JEDI ACADEMY IS CALLED A PRAXEUM, A PLACE FOR THE LEARNING OF ACTION.
USING EVERY RESOURCE AVAILABLE TO ME, I TRY TO TEACH THEM EVERYTHING OBI-WAN WOULD HAVE WANTED THEM TO KNOW.
"THEY LEARN TO FIGHT...
"...THEY LEARN TO THINK."
OUR ENEMIES HAVE FOUGHT AGAINST US IN MANY WAYS, BUT THE REBEL ALLIANCE--THE NEW REPUBLIC--HAS ALWAYS BEEN VICTORIOUS.

"BESIDES, I HAVE MY OWN WEAPONS... MY NEW JEDI KNIGHTS...
"KYP DURRON ...YOUNG AND IMPETUOUS-- MUCH LIKE ME WHEN I WAS HIS AGE.
"ONCE MY GREATEST STUDENT, THEN MY GREATEST ENEMY UNDER THE TUTELAGE OF THE SHADE OF EXAR KUN.
"HE HAS BEEN THROUGH MUCH... I BELIEVE KYP COULD BECOME THE GREATEST OF US ALL.
"KIRANA TI... A WARRIOR WOMAN, ONE OF THE WITCHES OF DATHOMIR.
"SHE HAS RIDDEN RANCORS, AND IS AN EXPERT IN THE PHYSICAL SIDE OF THE FORCE.
"STREEN... A HERMIT AND CLOUD PROSPECTOR I DISCOVERED ON BESPIN.
"HE DOESN'T LIKE PEOPLE, BUT HAS LEARNED TO OVERCOME HIS NEED FOR ISOLATION. HIS AFFINITY IS WITH THE WIND AND WEATHER.
"TIONNE... A JEDI LORE-MASTER AND HISTORIAN, FASCINATED WITH THE TALES OF THE JEDI. I FOUND HER RESCUING ARTIFACTS ON DOOMED EXIS STATION.
"SHE GIVES ME THE PERSPECTIVE I NEED TO UNDERSTAND OUR CHALLENGES IN THE CONTEXT OF THOUSANDS OF YEARS OF JEDI KNIGHTS."

BDEEP? DWIPP!
YES, ARTOO? I WAS JUST LOST IN THOUGHT.
THINKING OF ALL THE POTENTIAL, ALL THE POSSIBILITIES...
WE HAVE SURVIVED THE DEPREDATIONS OF THE EMPIRE--
--THE ATTACKS OF THRAWN AND DAALA--
--BUT WE CANNOT REST.
" YOU MUST LEARN WHAT YOU CAN, HERE AND ELSEWHERE.
" YOU WILL BECOME PALADINS OF THE NEW REPUBLIC, CHAMPIONS OF THE FORCE.
" BUT YOU CANNOT STAY HERE IN CONTEMPLATION ALL YOUR LIVES. YOU MUST GO ABROAD IN THE GALAXY.
" YOU HAVE THE GREATER BURDEN TO DO AS WELL AS TO LEARN... "
...FOR WE ARE JEDI KNIGHTS!

CORBOS--EXPERIMENTAL MINING COLONY.
A PREFABRICATED INDUSTRIAL CITY ERECTED IN THE BOWL OF A CRATER...
...WHERE HOPEFUL MINERS EXCAVATE THE ROCK WALLS FOR ORE AND CRYSTAL DEPOSITS.
BUT THE COST OF HAULING THEIR HARD-WON TREASURES TO TRADING STATIONS IN ORBIT EATS UP MOST OF THEIR PROFITS.

HURRY UP AND GET THOSE CHARGES PLANTED!
WE CAN MAKE ONE MORE GOOD BLAST BEFORE THE STORM FRONT HITS!
ONCE THE BLACK RAIN SEASON STARTS, THIS WHOLE CRATER WALL BECOMES UNSTABLE.
WE'D BETTER HOPE THIS ONE'S A LUCKY STRIKE.
I DRAGGED MY WHOLE FAMILY TO CORBOS, LOOKING FOR MY FORTUNE...
...AND ALL I GOT WERE DIRTY FINGER-NAILS!
DURING THE BLACK RAIN SEASON, WE'LL ALL BE STUCK INSIDE OUR DOMES.
PLENTY OF TIME WITH THE FAMILY, AT LEAST.
HEAVY CRYSTALLINE READINGS BEHIND THE WALL... UNUSUAL MINERAL TRACES.
I THINK WE MIGHT HAVE SOMETHING HERE.
HURRY UP!
OVER THE BARRICADE! THE TIMER'S ALREADY SET!
GET DOWN!

BROOOOOOOM!

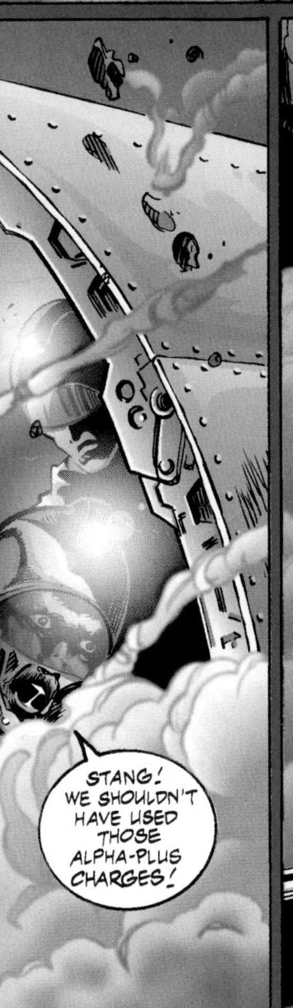
STANG! WE SHOULDN'T HAVE USED THOSE ALPHA-PLUS CHARGES!

GREAT... HALF THE CRATER WALL IS COMING DOWN!
WHO'S GOING TO CLEAN UP THIS MESS?

I'M NOT WAITING ALL DAY FOR THE SMOKE TO CLEAR.
LET'S TAKE A LOOK AND SEE WHAT WE'VE UN-COVERED.

IN THIRTY YEARS OF MINING, I'VE NEVER SEEN ANYTHING LIKE THIS!

IT'S A FOSSIL OF SOME KIND-- WHAT A BEAST!
SURE IS UGLY.
I WONDER WHAT KIND OF CREATURE IT WAS...
AN EXTINCT ONE, THAT'S ALL I CARE ABOUT!
"COME ON, CREW-- BACK TO THE DOMES. THE BLACK RAIN IS STARTING."
AAROOOOOO
WHAT WAS THAT?
I'M SURE IT WAS JUST THE STORM...

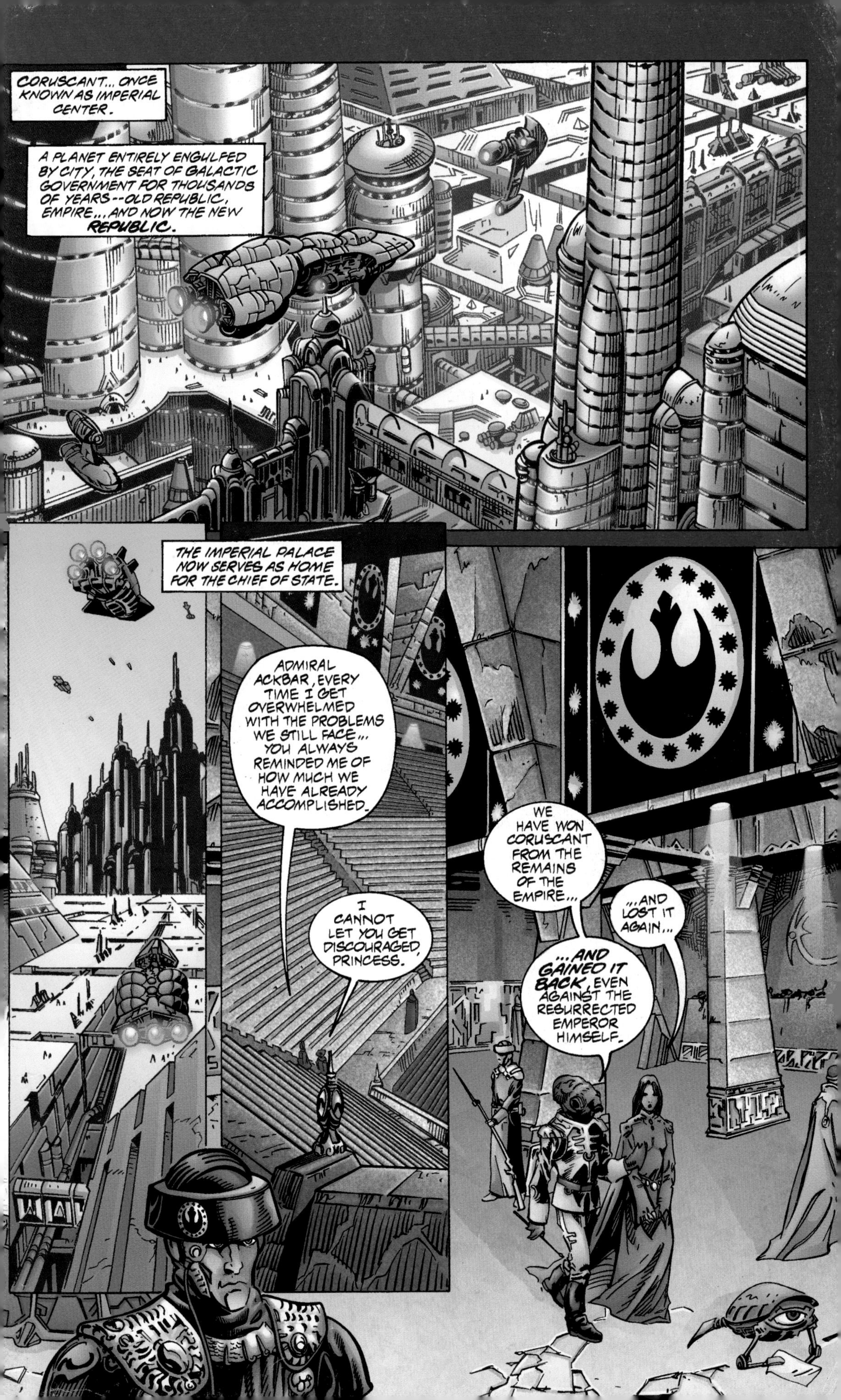
CORUSCANT... ONCE KNOWN AS IMPERIAL CENTER.
A PLANET ENTIRELY ENGULFED BY CITY, THE SEAT OF GALACTIC GOVERNMENT FOR THOUSANDS OF YEARS--OLD REPUBLIC, EMPIRE... AND NOW THE NEW REPUBLIC.
THE IMPERIAL PALACE NOW SERVES AS HOME FOR THE CHIEF OF STATE.
ADMIRAL ACKBAR, EVERY TIME I GET OVERWHELMED WITH THE PROBLEMS WE STILL FACE... YOU ALWAYS REMINDED ME OF HOW MUCH WE HAVE ALREADY ACCOMPLISHED.
I CANNOT LET YOU GET DISCOURAGED, PRINCESS.
WE HAVE WON CORUSCANT FROM THE REMAINS OF THE EMPIRE...
...AND LOST IT AGAIN...
...AND GAINED IT BACK, EVEN AGAINST THE RESURRECTED EMPEROR HIMSELF.

WE HAVE DEFEATED ADMIRAL DAALA TWICE. WE HAVE DESTROYED THE HUTTS' DARKSABER PROJECT.
YOUR BROTHER HAS TRAINED NEW JEDI KNIGHTS, WHO WILL ACT AS A STABILIZING INFLUENCE THROUGHOUT OUR WOUNDED REPUBLIC.
NOW I CAN SEE WHY MON MOTHMA DIDN'T WANT TO DO THIS JOB FOREVER.
CHIEF OF STATE, WE PIPED THROUGH AN URGENT TRANSMISSION! THE COMM CENTER THOUGHT YOU SHOULD SEE THIS YOURSELF.
WHY IS IT ALWAYS A CRISIS?
CORBOS... MINING COLONY! WE ARE UNDER ATTACK! SOME SORT OF... CREATURE.
DESTROYING OUR ENTIRE CITY! WE HAVE NO WEAPONS AGAINST--
SEND HELP-- PLEASE!
AND WHY DO I ALWAYS FEEL SO HELPLESS?
YOU CAN'T BE RESPONSIBLE FOR EVERY SENTIENT BEING IN THE GALAXY.
THOSE MINERS NEED HELP, ADMIRAL-- BUT I AM STILL REBUILDING THE MILITARY.
YOU KNOW WHAT A SHAMBLES THE FLEET IS IN... HOW CAN I SEND A FIGHTING FORCE?
MIGHT I SUGGEST YOU TAKE ADVANTAGE OF ALL YOUR RESOURCES, LEIA?
CALL LUKE. I'M SURE HE MIGHT HAVE A JEDI KNIGHT OR TWO WHO COULD GO TO CORBOS.
hmm...

YAVIN FOUR.
YOU CALLED ME, MASTER SKYWALKER?
THE SUPPLY SHIP IS ON ITS WAY DOWN FROM ORBIT.
IT'S GOT A PASSENGER ABOARD I WANT YOU TO MEET...
DEEP QRRLLL FWIP!
SOMEONE WHO WILL LOOK VERY FAMILIAR TO YOU, I THINK.
WELCOME TO MY JEDI ACADEMY.
DORSK 81? BUT YOU'RE--
DORSK 82, ACTUALLY. DON'T YOU REMEMBER ME FROM YOUR VISIT TO OUR CLONE PLANET KHOMM?
I'M HERE TO SEE IF I HAVE THE JEDI POTENTIAL THAT MY... PREDECESSOR EXHIBITED.

THANK YOU FOR TAKING ME TO THE GRAVE OF MY PREDECESSOR.
THIS IS A PILGRIMAGE I MUST MAKE...
JUST BE CAREFUL-- THE JUNGLE IS SOMETIMES A DANGEROUS PLACE.

DORSK 81 WAS A FRIEND OF MINE. HE FOUGHT WELL.
HIS BRAVERY AND HIS SACRIFICE SAVED THE ENTIRE JEDI ACADEMY DURING THE ATTACK BY ADMIRAL DAALA AND PELLAEON.
I COME OUT HERE MYSELF SOMETIMES, TO MEDITATE.
HERE IS HIS LIGHT-SABER.
HE PRIDED HIMSELF SO MUCH ON HIS JEDI TRAINING, EVEN THOUGH IT CAUSED MANY PROBLEMS FO HIS PREDECESSOR, DORSK 80.
IF YOU'RE GOING TO TRAIN HERE WITH US, YOU SHOULD TAKE HIS LIGHTSABER.
BUT I... DON'T EVEN KNOW IF I CAN USE THE FORCE.
MAYBE I SHOULD JUST LEAVE IT HERE...
KRISKK
I SENSE... LOOK OUT!

IT'S A MUTATED JUNGLE CREATURE-- BE CAREFUL OF THE VENOM!
"A DISTANT DESCENDANT OF EXAR KUN'S HANDIWORK... ITS BLOODLINE SURVIVED HERE FOR THOUSANDS OF YEARS."
...STAND BACK BEHIND ME. I'LL DEFEND YOU.
BUT I CAN TAKE CARE OF THIS...

THANKS. ALL I COULD DO WAS COWER. I WAS DEFENSE-LESS.
IT'S THE LEAST I COULD DO FOR THE MEMORY OF DORSK 81.
I WANT TO LEARN HOW TO FIGHT LIKE THAT!
THEN I'LL HELP YOU TO BECOME A JEDI-- BUT DON'T EXPECT IT TO BE EASY!

JEDI ACADEMY COMMUNICATIONS CENTER -- THE TACTICAL ROOM OF THE FORMER REBEL BASE.
LEIA, GOOD TO HEAR FROM YOU--WHAT'S WRONG? I CAN SENSE HOW TROUBLED YOU ARE.
WE NEED YOUR HELP, LUKE--AND THE HELP OF YOUR NEW JEDI TRAINEES.
I RECEIVED AN EMERGENCY MESSAGE FROM A GROUP OF MINERS ON CORBOS-- A WORLD THAT'S EVEN MORE ISOLATED THAN YAVIN FOUR.
IF THAT'S POSSIBLE!
THEY'RE UNDER SOME KIND OF ATTACK, BUT THE TRANSMISSION CUT OFF. I DON'T KNOW WHAT'S HAPPENING, AND I CAN'T SPARE PART OF THE FLEET TO INVESTIGATE.
YOU'RE NOT FAR FROM CORBOS, LUKE.
DO YOU THINK ONE OF YOUR STUDENTS COULD CHECK THIS OUT? CAN THEY HANDLE IT?
LEIA, I CAN'T THINK OF A BETTER WAY FOR THEM TO LEARN.

I HAVE CALLED YOU HERE BECAUSE WE HAVE WORK TO DO...
...THE WORK OF A JEDI KNIGHT.
WE HAVE LITTLE INFORMATION-- A MINING COLONY UNDER ATTACK.
I BELIEVE ONE OF YOU CAN INVESTIGATE.
KYP DURRON, I WOULD LIKE YOU TO FLY TO CORBOS. HELP THE MINERS, IF YOU CAN.
I WANT TO TAKE DORSK 82 WITH ME.
I WAS HOPING YOU WOULD SUGGEST THAT...
ONCE YOU ARRIVE ON CORBOS, ASSESS THE SITUATION.
IF YOU CAN'T HANDLE IT YOURSELF, I WANT YOU TO SUMMON STREEN AND KIRANA TI.
IF I DO NEED HELP, I CAN THINK OF NO ONE ELSE I'D RATHER HAVE BY MY SIDE... OTHER THAN YOU, MASTER SKYWALKER.
SO WE JUST WAIT HERE? AND KEEP TRAINING?
THERE WILL BE OTHER MISSIONS FOR ALL OF YOU. IN THIS WAY, WE CAN HELP PROVIDE A STABLE FOUNDATION FOR THE NEW REPUBLIC.
THE DARK SIDE ALWAYS PROVIDES ENOUGH WORK TO KEEP US BUSY...

TAKE THIS SHIP, THE CELADOR SASH, DONATED TO US BY A GRATEFUL TRADER. APPARENTLY OBI-WAN KENOBI SAVED HIS PARENTS ONCE, A LONG TIME AGO.
IT'S AN OUTDATED DESIGN, BUT STILL PERFECTLY SERVICEABLE.
DO YOU THINK WE CAN FLY IT?
THIS IS TERRIFIC-- JUST WHAT WE NEED.
IT SMELLS MUSTY IN HERE...
DON'T WORRY--YOU'LL HAVE PLENTY OF TIME TO CLEAN IT WHILE WE'RE IN HYPER-SPACE.
THOSE MINERS ARE WAITING!
I'M NOT TRAINED ON THIS KIND OF CONTROL PANEL... I WAS INSTRUCTED TO HELP MANAGE THE CLONING FACILITIES ON KHOMM--
YOU CAN LEARN, DORSK 82. THE FUEL PODS ARE FULLY CHARGED. THAT'S ALL I NEED TO KNOW.
MAY THE FORCE BE WITH YOU.
DO YOU THINK HE'LL CALL FOR HELP IF HE NEEDS IT?
KYP DURRON? NOT A CHANCE-- NOT WILLING-LY.

HERE, LET ME HELP YOU WITH THE COURSE-SETTING DISPLAY.
STANDARD EQUIPMENT, MODIFIED NAVICOMPUTER WITH THREE-DIMENSIONAL HOLOGRAPHIC MAP EXTENSION...
TRACK DOWN CORBOS AND LAY IN A DIRECT COURSE...
BUT... BUT I'M NOT EVEN SURE THIS IS CORBOS. ARE YOU CERTAIN THIS IS A SAFE ROUTE, KYP? PLEASE DOUBLE CHECK MY--
DORSK 82, WE CAN'T WASTE ANY MORE TIME. I TRUST IN YOUR ABILITIES.
HERE WE GO INTO HYPER-SPACE!
BUT I DON'T TRUST IN MY ABILITIES, KYP! I DON'T KNOW WHY I EVEN CAME TO THE JEDI ACADEMY.
MY GENETIC LINE HAS HAD EIGHTY-TWO GENERATIONS, AND ONLY ONE HAS EVER BECOME A JEDI.
"IF DORSK 81 HAD IT, THEN ALL OF YOU MUST HAVE HAD THE POTENTIAL.
"BUT HE ALSO HAD HIS DOUBTS. HE AND I WENT ON MISSIONS TOGETHER. WE EXPOSED ADMIRAL DAALA'S PLANS, HER ALLIANCE WITH PELLAEON.
"BUT WE BOTH CAME BACK TO YAVIN FOUR TO DEFEND THE JEDI ACADEMY. ALL THE NEW JEDI KNIGHTS FOUGHT TOGETHER, BUT ONLY DORSK 81 HAD THE BRAVERY AND THE SKILL TO SAVE THE JUNGLE MOON.
"WE ALL FOUGHT, BUT HE USED THE FORCE MORE THAN ANY OF US. HE JOINED HIMSELF WITH THE OTHER TRAINEES. HE DREW UPON EVERYTHING, OPENED EVERY CELL OF HIS BODY TO THE FORCE--AND UNLEASHED IT!
"HIS ONE EFFORT DROVE BACK PELLAEON'S ENTIRE FLEET OF STAR DESTROYERS... SHOVING THEM HALFWAY THROUGH THE YAVIN SYSTEM."
BUT THAT PROVED TOO MUCH FOR HIM. THE POWER HE USED... BURNED HIMSELF OUT, AND HE DIED.
NOW DON'T TALK TO ME ANY MORE NONSENSE THAT YOU HAVE NO SKILLS!

CORBOS...
WELL, WE MADE IT TO CORBOS EXPERIMENTAL MINING COLONY--GARDEN SPOT OF THE OUTER RIM.
GOOD NAVIGATING, DORSK 82.
KYP--WHAT'S THIS? A DISTRESS SIGNAL?
IT SEEMS TO BE AUTOMATED.
THIS IS KYP DURRON, JEDI KNIGHT, CALLING CORBOS MINING COLONY.
WE ARE RESPONDING TO YOUR DISTRESS SIGNAL TO THE NEW REPUBLIC.
"HOW CAN WE BE OF ASSISTANCE? PLEASE COME IN!"
THE EXCAVATORS ARE INSIDE THOSE CRATERS!
THE MINERS TUNNEL INTO THE WALLS, WHERE GEOLOGIC UPHEAVAL HAS MIXED THE MINERALS AND CRYSTALS NEAR THE SURFACE.
EVEN WITH THAT BLACK RAIN, THE PLACE SURE LOOKS DESOLATE.

LOOK AT THAT DEVASTATION! IT'S LIKE A WAR TOOK PLACE HERE!
THIS WAS JUST A PEACEFUL MINING COLONY, NOT VERY PROFITABLE, EITHER.
WE'VE GOT TO TAKE A CLOSER LOOK, DORSK 82.

KYP, ARE YOU ALL RIGHT?
CAN YOU HEAR THAT? SCREAMING... CRIES FOR HELP...

...INSIDE MY HEAD, ALL OF THEM... SO MANY PEOPLE, SO MANY VOICES... CRYING OUT THROUGH THE FORCE.

I CAN'T HEAR ANYTHING. MAYBE BECAUSE I HAVEN'T BEEN TRAINED...
...OR MAYBE BECAUSE I HAVE NO POTENTIAL FOR USING THE FORCE.

THERE WERE THIRTY FAMILIES DOWN IN THE CRATER CITY. I CAN HEAR THEIR... DESPAIR AND TERROR.
IT'S ABSOLUTELY RELENT-LESS.

YOU'RE LANDING? ARE YOU SURE IT'S SAFE?
YOU NEED TO LEARN TO TRUST YOUR OWN INSTINCTS AND YOUR OWN RESOURCES, DORSK 82.
BUT... SHOULDN'T WE CALL IN THE REINFORCEMENTS? STREEN, KIRANA TI? WE PROMISED THEM WE'D ASK FOR HELP.
I WANT TO LOOK AROUND FIRST... ANSWER A FEW QUESTIONS OF MY OWN.
I CAN'T IMAGINE HOW ANYONE COULD HAVE SURVIVED THIS KIND OF ATTACK.
BUT EVEN THIS STORM CAN'T DROWN OUT THE SCREAMING IN MY HEAD...

WE'LL TAKE THESE SUPPLIES FROM THE SHIP. YOU NEVER KNOW WHAT WE MIGHT NEED.
I THINK WE NEED THE NEW REPUBLIC MILITARY FLEET!
I THINK YOU NEED MORE CONFIDENCE, DORSK 82...
...IF YOU WANT TO BECOME A JEDI.

THIS SEALED DOOR DIDN'T HOLD FOR LONG.
IT WAS NEVER MEANT TO KEEP OUT WHATEVER ATTACKED HERE.
DO YOU FEEL LIKE WE'RE BEING WATCHED?
I SENSE MANY PRESENCES... ALL AROUND...
"...ALL AFRAID..."
"...ALL IN PAIN."
WHA--?
YAAAH! DORSK 82, LOOK OUT!
VVMMM
SOME-ONE SHOULD FIX THAT LEAK.

THIS IS--WAS THE CENTRAL CONTROL ROOM.
DO YOU THINK WE'LL FIND A LOG, OR SOME RECORD OF WHAT HAPPENED?
ALL THE SYSTEMS ARE SMASHED.
ALL THAT BLOOD.
WE KNOW AT LEAST SOME OF THEM DIED... AND THEY DIDN'T DIE CLEANLY, EITHER...
I'M SURPRISED THEY MANAGED TO GET ANY MESSAGE OUT AT ALL.
BLASTER MARKS... LOTS OF THEM.
THE MINERS HAD ENOUGH FIREPOWER... BUT IT DIDN'T DO THEM ANY GOOD.

IF... SOMETHING KILLED ALL THE COLONISTS, WHAT CHANCE DO WE HAVE?
THERE ARE ONLY TWO OF US.

YES, BUT WE HAVE THE FORCE ON OUR SIDE... AND IT IS A POWERFUL ALLY.
BUT NOBODY SAID IT'S GOING TO BE EASY.

COME ON--LET'S LOOK AROUND SOME MORE.

THEY LEFT THEIR MINING TOOLS JUST LYING AROUND.
NOT JUST LYING HERE--SEE, THEY'RE SPLINTERED AND BENT. AS IF THEY USED THEM AS... WEAPONS.
WE MUST BE GETTING CLOSE TO THE MINERS' QUARTERS. THOSE USED TO BE LOCKERS FOR PERSONAL POSSESSIONS.
WHAT-EVER ATTACKED HERE WASN'T SEARCHING FOR ANYTHING... IT JUST WANTED TO DESTROY.

HELLLOO! IS ANYONE ALIVE IN HERE?
YOU DON'T EXPECT AN ANSWER, DO YOU? WHAT ARE WE GOING TO DO?

THESE ARE THE FAMILY UNITS.
LOOKS JUST AS DEVASTATED IN HERE.

IT WAS A CHILD'S ROOM, I THINK.

WHAT'S THIS? A DERBIT CASE?

RECORDS SHOW 793 MINERS AND THEIR FAMILIES LIVED HERE ON CORBOS.

AFTER SEEING THIS, I DOUBT WE'LL FIND ANY OF THEM ALIVE.

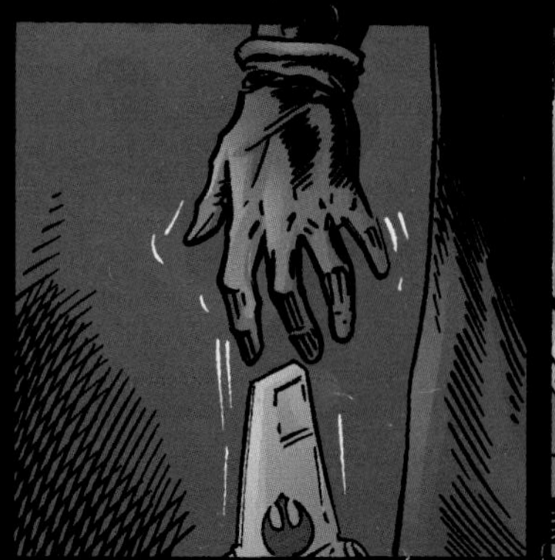

KRSH

IT'S AT THE EDGE OF MY PERCEPTION... I STILL SENSE SOMETHING, NAGGING AT ME.
IF THE MINERS ARE ALL DEAD, WHY DO I STILL HEAR SO MANY WHISPERS IN MY MIND?
LOOK, KYP-- I FOUND A CHRONO-METER...
...ACCORDING TO THIS, IT'LL BE LOCAL DAYLIGHT IN ONLY A FEW HOURS.
WE'LL WAIT OUT THE STORM HERE. SLEEP IF YOU CAN.
SLEEP? IN THIS PLACE?
I DON'T THINK WE'RE IN TIME FOR ANY RESCUE... BUT WE'VE STILL GOT A MYSTERY TO SOLVE.
WE OWE IT TO THOSE MINERS.

THE NIGHT IS DARK AND BROODING, AND THIS ENTIRE PLACE IS A NIGHTMARE.
WITH HIS JEDI SENSES STILL NOT FULLY AWAKENED, DORSK 82 CAN SEE ONLY THE TANGIBLE TERRORS AROUND HIM...
...THUS, HE CAN SLEEP.
BUT I CAN SENSE SO MUCH MORE.
TNK
TNK
THERE IS SOMETHING OUT THERE.
I KNOW IT.
AND IT IS COMING CLOSER.
THE VOICES IN MY HEAD HAVE COME BACK SCREAMING... WAILING!

THE FORCE MAKES ME HEAR THEM... I CAN NOT IGNORE THEIR CRIES.
I AM A JEDI KNIGHT!
GOING OUT TO FACE THAT THING IS TOO DANGEROUS FOR YOU, MY FRIEND.
I SHOULD NEVER HAVE BROUGHT YOU INTO THIS.
I HAVE TO DO THIS ALONE.
I HAVE TO HELP.
READY OR NOT, HERE I COME.

YAVIN 4

KYP AND DORSK 82 HAVE ARRIVED ON CORBOS BY NOW.
NO WORD FROM THEM YET.

I HEAR THERE ARE MANY STORMS ON CORBOS.
WE DON'T KNOW MUCH AT ALL ABOUT THAT PLACE.

IN FACT, WITH THE VARIOUS RECORDS AND DATABASES I HAVE IN MY QUARTERS, I WONDER IF I CAN LEARN ANYTHING MORE ABOUT CORBOS.

PERHAPS I CAN LEARN SOMETHING USEFUL.

IF KYP DURRON NEEDED HELP, I DOUBT HE WOULD ASK.

TIME TO GET TO WORK... THERE SHOULD BE SOME INFORMATION IN ALL THIS!
MAYBE THIS OLD HOLOCRON CAN GIVE ME A FEW CLUES.
AND LET'S SEE WHAT THE MAIN NEW REPUBLIC GALACTIC DATA-BASE HAS TO SAY ABOUT CORBOS.
EARLY SETTLEMENT ATTEMPTS DATE BACK THOUSANDS AND THOUSANDS OF YEARS.
NOTHING MUCH REMARKABLE ABOUT THE SYSTEM ITSELF, A FEW MODERATELY VALUABLE ROCKS
THE TEXT IS ARCHAIC, BUT I CAN SEE THAT CORBOS WAS DESIRABLE ONLY TO THOSE WHO DON'T HAVE ANY OTHER PLACE TO GO.
THAT'S VERY ODD...

"THESE RECORDS DON'T OVERLAP VERY WELL. I DOUBT ANYONE HAS NOTICED THE PAST HISTORY.
"CORBOS HAS BEEN SETTLED MANY TIMES OVER THE MILLENNIA.
"COLONY AFTER COLONY, WITH CENTURIES IN BETWEEN. THE SYSTEM IS OUT OF THE WAY... ISOLATED.
"NO ONE HAS PAID ANY ATTENTION TO THE PLACE.
"BUT IN EVERY INSTANCE, THE COLONY WAS DESTROYED.
"ALL THE MINERS VANISHED.
"NO SURVIVORS... AND NO EXPLANATIONS."
KYP AND DORSK 82 DON'T KNOW WHAT THEY'RE GETTING INTO.

CORBOS
I'M ALONE! IS HE DEAD, TOO?
KYP!! WHERE ARE YOU?

HE'S NOT HERE!

GOT TO GET BACK TO THE SHIP, USE THE COMM SYSTEM...

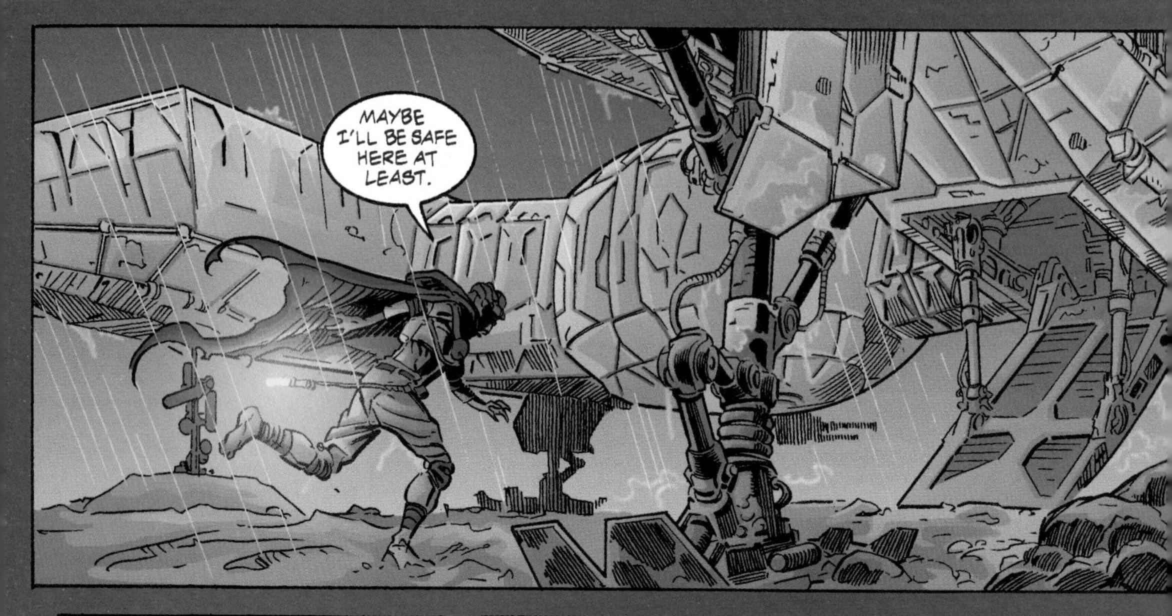
MAYBE I'LL BE SAFE HERE AT LEAST.

CAN'T SEE ANY SIGN OF HIM... I WISH HE'D LEFT SOME KIND OF WARNING, SOME KIND OF MESSAGE.
OH, KYP...

THIS IS DORSK 82, CALLING YAVIN 4 - MASTER SKYWALKER-- JEDI ACADEMY, PLEASE RESPOND! WE REQUIRE URGENT ASSISTANCE.

A JEDI KNOWS WHEN TO BE ALONE... AND WHEN TO BE BRAVE ENOUGH TO CALL FOR HELP.

IT'S UP THERE. I CAN SENSE THE SCREAMS.
THAT'S WHERE THE MINERS WENT.
OR AT LEAST THAT'S WHERE I CAN FIND THE ANSWER TO THIS MYSTERY.
WHATEVER HAPPENS, I NEED TO KNOW.

NOT VERY STABLE AROUND HERE...
HERE... SOMETHING HAPPENED HERE.

SOMETHING AWAKENED.
A MISTAKE...
THE MINERS HAD NO IDEA... NO DEFENSE.
THEY DIDN'T HAVE A CHANCE.
BUT THEY'RE STILL HERE.
AARROOOOOOOOO
UP THERE...

YAVIN 4
IT'S KYP DURRON... I KNEW THERE WOULD BE TROUBLE!
HE SHOULD HAVE BROUGHT US ALONG IN THE FIRST PLACE.
BDEEP DWIPP!
GOOD THING WE'RE PREPARED.
MASTER SKYWALKER GAVE US THE SHIP. I ALREADY TOOK THE LIBERTY OF SETTING THE COORDINATES FOR CORBOS...
...JUST IN CASE.
IF A JEDI NEEDS OUR HELP, THERE IS NO TIME TO LOSE.

HOW MUCH ACCELERATION CAN YOU ENDURE, STREEN?
AS MUCH AS I HAVE TO.

CORBOS
THIS MONSTER... THIS LEVIATHAN CAME IN THE NIGHT. ONCE IT ATTACKED THE FIRST MINER, IT SOMEHOW GAINED HIS KNOWLEDGE. IT ASSIMILATED EVERYTHING HE KNEW, EVERYTHING HE WAS. AND THEN IT KNEW EXACTLY HOW TO DESTROY THE ENTIRE COLONY.
ALL THE WEAKNESSES. EVERY HIDING PLACE. AND THE LEVIATHAN DIDN'T STOP UNTIL IT HAD DEVOURED EVERY LAST SCREAM.

ALL THE MINERS ARE DEAD... I KNOW THAT NOW.
BUT PERHAPS IT ISN'T TOO LATE.

GOT TO GET TO THE TOP... WHERE THE VOICES ARE.

THERE YOU ARE.
FZZSSH

WE'VE GOT A SCORE TO SETTLE, YOU AND I!

COME AND GET ME, MONSTER.

UNARMED COLONISTS ARE ONE THING...
...BUT NOW YOU'RE FIGHTING A JEDI!
AARRRGH

IN THE RUINS OF CORBOS MINING CITY...
FINALLY... THEY'RE HERE AT LAST!
STREEN! KIRANA TI! AM I GLAD TO SEE YOU!
KYP'S GONE TO FIND THE MONSTER THAT KILLED ALL THE COLONISTS.
I'M AFRAID FOR HIM. HE CAN'T POSSIBLY FIGHT THAT CREATURE ALL ALONE.
THEN WE WILL HAVE TO GO FIND HIM.

CAN'T THE OVERLANDER GO ANY FASTER?
THE STORM MAKES EVERYTHING MORE DIFFICULT.

IS THAT ITS FOOTPRINT? IT'S HUGE!

THIS IS LARGER THAN THE RANCORS I HAVE FOUGHT... AND RIDDEN... ON DATHOMIR.

BUT KYP IS STILL ALIVE... I SENSE IT.

THIS LEADS INTO THE TUNNELS THE MINERS EXCAVATED.

MAYBE THEY UNCOVERED SOMETHING THEY SHOULDN'T HAVE.

WHAT'S THIS?

"I HEAR THEM SCREAMING..."
I MUST SET THEM FREE.
KRSHH!

AHH!

A JEDI IS NEVER WITHOUT A WEAPON...

INSIDE THE MINE TUNNELS...
THIS MUST HAVE BEEN THE MAIN GENERATOR COMPLEX FOR THE MINES.
NOT THAT IT'S NEEDED NOW.
THIS WHOLE CRATER MUST BE VOLCANIC IN ORIGIN.
A GOOD HEAT EXCHANGER CAN CONVERT ENORMOUS POWER DIRECTLY FROM THE LAVA.
COME ON. LET'S FIND KYP.

WHERE DO WE GO NOW? THIS PLACE IS A MAZE.
YOU HAVE TOO MANY DOUBTS FOR A JEDI, DORSK 82.
WE FOLLOW THE FORCE.
I'VE HAD ENOUGH JEDI TRAINING TO SENSE DANGER.
THERE'S SOMETHING VERY DANGEROUS IN HERE...
...BUT IT ISN'T NECESSARILY THE THING KYP IS FIGHTING.
WE'RE PREPARED.

I SENSE SOMETHING DARK HERE... SOMETHING EVIL, AND HUNGRY.
DO YOU THINK ONE OF THE COLONISTS ACCIDENTALLY --

NO, THIS IS NOT WHAT KYP IS FIGHTING.
I THINK HE'S UP AGAINST SOMETHING EVEN WORSE.

WHAT ARE YOU LOOKING AT?
I DON'T LIKE BEING STARED AT!
HAH!

NOW I'VE LOST MY WEAPON... BUT I'M STILL NOT HELPLESS.
I CAN USE THIS STORM. LIKE STREEN CAN CONTROL THE WEATHER.
WITH THE FORCE, I CAN CALL DOWN...

...THE LIGHTNING!

WE'VE BEEN CLIMBING UPHILL FOR A LONG TIME.
WE'RE GETTING CLOSER.
YES. THIS IS THE PLACE.
LISTEN... I HEAR THE STORM. AND FIGHTING.

KYP! WE'RE COMING!

WELL, THAT WAS EASY ENOUGH.
BUT THE SCREAMING HASN'T STOPPED IN MY HEAD.
THE COLONISTS, OR WHATEVER'S LEFT OF THEM, ARE STILL TRAPPED.

UNTIL I SET THEM FREE.

MAYBE NOW IT'LL BE QUIET.

THERE HE IS!
HE'S ALIVE.
KYP DURRON! YOU'VE FINISHED THE FIGHT WITHOUT US.
I FOUND YOUR LIGHTSABER, KYP... THOUGH IT LOOKS LIKE YOU DID JUST FINE WITHOUT IT.
THAT'S THE UGLIEST THING I'VE EVER SEEN.
BUT IT'S DEAD NOW.
THE SOUNDS ARE QUIETER NOW... BUT WHY DO I STILL HEAR THE SCREAMING?
MORE VOICES, MORE TORMENT.
AAARRROOOOOO!

IT LOOKS LIKE WE'VE GOT AN EVEN BIGGER FIGHT AHEAD OF US...

AAARRRRROOOOOOOOOO!

LOOK OUT!
GET READY TO FIGHT, JEDI. I HAVE A FEELING THIS ONE WILL BE EVEN HARDER TO KILL.
I AM ALWAYS READY TO FIGHT.
I WISH MASTER SKYWALKER WERE HERE...

GGNNRRRR

BEFORE YOU USE YOUR LIGHTSABERS, LET ME MOVE THE WIND. THE STORM IS MY ALLY.
"I CAN HEAR THE COLONISTS, UNABLE TO DIE,...FEEDING THIS MONSTER WITH THEIR SCREAMS."
STREEN, WE MUST USE EVERY WEAPON WE HAVE.
"WE MUST FREE THEM!"

MAYBE THIS WILL MAKE AN IMPACT.
KCHING
COME HERE, LEVIATHAN!
IF YOU'VE HAD YOUR FILL OF TERRIFIED COLONISTS, TRY FIGHTING THE JEDI KNIGHTS!

HANG ON! WE'VE GOT TO BRING THIS THING DOWN!
GOT IT!
WHOA, MAYBE NOT!
ENOUGH OF THIS--IT'S TIME FOR LIGHTSABERS!

THIS IS MUCH BIGGER THAN THE LAST ONE--
THUD
WATCH OUT! THE PLATEAU'S CRACKING! THE GROUND IS OPENING UP!
RRRRROOOAARR!
HEY!
GRAB THE ROPES!

YAVIN 4.
STORM SEASON.

I HAVE TRAINED MANY STUDENTS. IT HAS BEEN MY QUEST TO BRING BACK THE JEDI KNIGHTS...
...TO DEFEND THE NEW REPUBLIC, MUCH AS THEY DID IN THE PAST.
I HAVE LOST MANY STUDENTS ALONG THE WAY.

AND I WILL LOSE MANY MORE.

BWEEP! BDOOOOO.

YOU'RE RIGHT, ARTOO. LET'S GET OUT OF THE RAIN. PLENTY OF WORK TO DO.
I CAN'T SPEND ALL DAY WORRYING ABOUT KYP AND THE OTHERS.

TIONNE HAS UNCOVERED THE HISTORY OF THIS MONSTER ON CORBOS. BUT NO SUGGESTIONS, NO SOLUTIONS.

I WISH I COULD HELP THEM FIGHT.

BUT MY PLACE IS HERE WITH THE OTHER TRAINEES, HELPING THEM TO BECOME STRONG.
THESE ARE THE NEXT GENERATION, THE ONLY WAY THE JEDI KNIGHTS WILL BE REBORN IN THE GALAXY.

FTTZLSHHH
UHHH! GOT IT!

I THINK WE'D BETTER GET DOWN... BEFORE WE FALL.
WATCH OUT FOR THE LAVA!
BLOOP
I'M GOING TO NEED A LITTLE HELP!
DORSK 82, CATCH THIS ROPE AND TIE IT ON SO I CAN GET ACROSS!
GOT IT!
CATCH!
I'VE GOT YOU, KYP!

HEADS UP!
MADE IT!

NO SIGN OF THAT CREATURE.
DO YOU THINK IT'S DEAD?

NO... THE SCREAMING STILL ECHOES IN MY HEAD. CAN'T YOU HEAR IT?

WE DIDN'T GET HERE IN TIME TO SAVE THE COLONISTS...
...WE BARELY MANAGED TO SAVE OURSELVES.

WAIT! LOOK! SOMETHING'S HAPPENING!

HHHRAAROOO

LOOK OUT! I'LL TRY TO DIVERT SOME OF IT!

NOT AGAIN! THIS THING IS CAUSING SOME SERIOUS PROBLEMS!
AND NOW IT'S EVEN UGLIER THAN BEFORE!

I SUPPOSE THE COLONISTS DIDN'T PUT UP MUCH OF A FIGHT.

I DON'T THINK THIS BEAST IS RECEPTIVE TO LEARNING ITS LESSON.

WE'VE HAD TOUGHER CHALLENGES... I THINK.

I WISH I COULD HELP. IT'S HARD ENOUGH JUST TO DODGE THOSE LAVA DROPS.
I HOPE THIS POWER GENERATOR GIVES ENOUGH PROTECTION. IT WAS DESIGNED TO FUNCTION NEXT TO THE LAVA...

AND IT'S STILL WORKING!
HEY, THIS GENERATOR PROVIDED POWER TO THE WHOLE COLONY, AND THE MINING INDUSTRY--

KYP! WE CAN USE THE GENERATOR!

THE CABLES ARE STILL INTACT!

WITH A POWER SURGE, WE CAN FRY THE MONSTER...
UH, IF YOU CAN SOMEHOW CONNECT THE CABLES TO IT.

SURE, GO GET THE CABLES.

I CAN KEEP THIS THING BUSY.
FOR A SECOND OR TWO.

GET EVERYTHING READY. I DON'T THINK A LIGHTSABER OR TWO IS GOING TO STOP IT.

YAAAAAAAHH!
STAY BY THE CONTROLS, DORSK 82. KEEP THE POWER OFF UNTIL WE'RE READY.
BUT DON'T WAIT TOO LONG!

EVERYBODY OFF! GET OUT OF HERE!
RUN! COVER YOUR EYES!
FULL POWER... NOW!

ZZZZAATT!

LOOK, THEY'RE FREE!

WE DID IT! THAT'S ALL OF THEM!

I THINK... I THINK I CAN HEAR IT.

ALL I HEAR NOW IS SILENCE... PEACEFUL, BLESSED SILENCE IN MY HEAD.

CORBOS IS DEAD... JUST A HOME FOR THE WIND... AND NOTHING MORE.
I DON'T KNOW WHAT THE MINERS DID TO AWAKEN THOSE CREATURES.
I SURE HOPE THERE AREN'T ANY MORE.
I FEEL LIKE WE SUCCEEDED AND FAILED AT THE SAME TIME.
SOMETIMES IT'S HARD TO TELL THE DIFFERENCE BETWEEN FAILURE AND SUCCESS.
ALL THOSE PEOPLE...
SEE YOU BACK AT YAVIN 4.

YAVIN 4.
DORSK 81... MY PREDECESSOR. A JEDI HERO. YOU SAVED THE ACADEMY HERE. YOU FELT THE FORCE.
I'M YOUR CLONE. I SHOULD BE IDENTICAL. MAYBE I FEEL THE FORCE MOVING WITHIN ME, TOO. MAYBE.
I HOPE SO, BECAUSE I HAVE DECIDED THAT I WANT TO BECOME A JEDI.
IF THERE'S A WAY FOR YOU TO LEARN, I'LL HELP YOU IN EVERY WAY I CAN.
AFTER ALL, WE CAN NEVER HAVE TOO MANY JEDI KNIGHTS!
END

KEVIN J. ANDERSON has written twenty-six best-selling novels, with over eleven million books in print in twenty-five languages. Though best known for his numerous *Star Wars* and *X-Files* projects, Anderson's original work has appeared on "Best of the Year" lists from *Locus*, *Science Fiction Chronicle*, and *SFX* magazines, the final ballots for the Nebula, the Bram Stoker Award, and the American Physics Society's Forum Award. In 1998, he set the Guinness World Record for "Largest Single-Author Book Signing" in Hollywood, CA. Anderson's current project is writing a prequel trilogy to Frank Herbert's *Dune*, co-authored with Herbert's son Brian and based on thousands of pages of recently discovered notes. *Dune: House Atreides* became an international bestseller and appeared on numerous "Best of the Year" lists. The second volume, *House Harkonnen*, will be published in October, 2000. *Jedi Academy — Leviathan* is the latest of Anderson's forays into the *Star Wars* comics mythos, his previous works including four *Tales of the Jedi* series: *Dark Lords of the Sith*, *The Sith War*, *The Golden Age of the Sith*, and *The Fall of the Sith Empire*.

DARIO CARRASCO, JR.'s intricate illustrations and complex designs are well known to *Star Wars* comics readers, his work having previously been featured in a troika of *Tales of the Jedi* series: *The Sith War*, *The Golden Age of the Sith*, and *The Fall of the Sith Empire*. *Jedi Academy* is Dario's fourth *Star Wars* teaming with longtime *Tales of the Jedi* writer Kevin J. Anderson. Dario has also pencilled a number of projects for Marvel Comics — including *Alpha Flight*, *Pinhead*, *Nova*, *What If?*, *Captain America*, and *Night Thrasher* — and is now drawing *Golden Crickets* for an independent publication in Alberta, Canada. A 1988 graduate of the Savannah College of Art and Design, Dario is currently employed as a structural designer for an engineering firm and lives in the countryside of Maple Ridge, British Columbia with his wife and three daughters.

MARK HEIKE has pencilled and/or inked for nearly every major American comics publisher on such titles as *Nexus*, *The Green Hornet*, *Wolverine*, *She-Hulk*, *Star Trek*, *Aliens vs. Predator*, *Mantra*, *Teenage Mutant Ninja Turtles*, *Xena: Warrior Princess*, *Secret Weapons*, *Magneto*, and *Spyboy*. He is perhaps best known for his work pencilling and inking over 100 issues of AC's *Femforce*, for which Mark is currently working on a revival. *Jedi Academy* is Mark's latest incursion into *Star Wars* space, having previously shared inking duties on three *Tales of the Jedi* series, *The Sith War*, *The Golden Age of the Sith*, and *The Fall of the Sith Empire*. Mark shares a Florida studio with his wife, Stephanie, and longtime associate Bill Black and is currently an associate editor on AC Comics' line of Golden Age and Western historical reprints.

GALLERY

Featuring the original comic-book series cover paintings by Ray Lago and Paul Chadwick

Ray Lago

Paul Chadwick

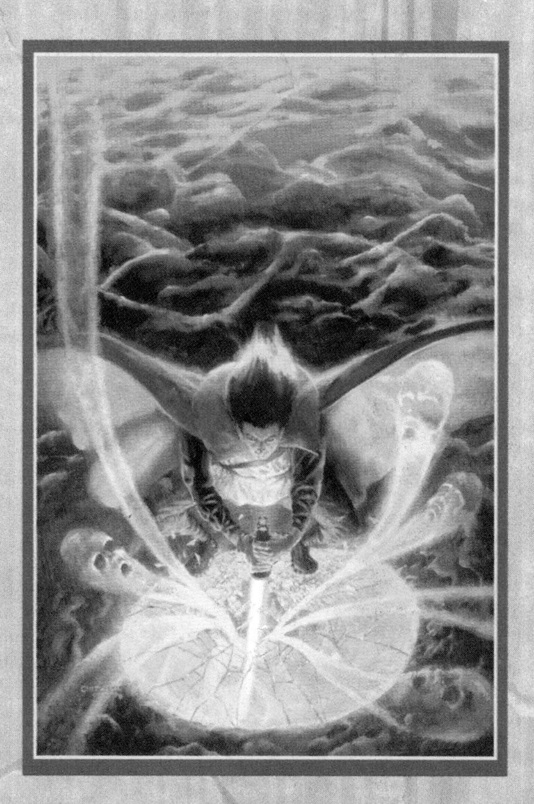

Paul Chadwick

Paul Chadwick

STAR WARS TRADE PAPERBACKS FROM DARK HORSE

CLASSIC STAR WARS
The classic newspaper strips, colored and enhanced.

VOLUME ONE: IN DEADLY PURSUIT
Goodwin • Williamson
ISBN: 1-56971-109-7 $16.95

VOLUME TWO: THE REBEL STORM
Goodwin • Williamson
ISBN: 1-56971-106-2 $16.95

VOLUME THREE: ESCAPE TO HOTH
Goodwin • Williamson
ISBN: 1-56971-093-7 $16.95

VOLUME FOUR: THE EARLY ADVENTURES
Manning • Hoberg
ISBN: 1-56971-178-X $19.95

VOLUME FIVE: HAN SOLO AT STARS' END
Goodwin • Alcala
ISBN: 1-56971-254-9 $6.95

MOVIE ADAPTATIONS

EPISODE 1–THE PHANTOM MENACE
Gilroy • Damaggio • Williamson
ISBN: 1-56971-359-6 $12.95

EPISODE 1– THE PHANTOM MENACE ADVENTURES
ISBN: 1-56971-443-6 $12.95

A NEW HOPE
Jones • Barreto • Williamson
ISBN: 1-56971-213-1 $9.95

THE EMPIRE STRIKES BACK
Goodwin • Williamson
ISBN: 1-56971-234-4 $9.95

RETURN OF THE JEDI
Goodwin • Williamson
ISBN: 1-56971-235-2 $9.95

THE STAR WARS TRILOGY: SPECIAL EDITION BOXED SET
Jones • Goodwin • Williamson • Garzón
ISBN: 1-56971-257-3 $29.85

MANGA EDITIONS
Translated into English

A NEW HOPE
George Lucas • Hisao Tamaki
VOLUME 1
ISBN: 1-56971-362-6 $9.95
VOLUME 2
ISBN: 1-56971-363-4 $9.95
VOLUME 3
ISBN: 1-56971-364-2 $9.95
VOLUME 4
ISBN: 1-56971-365-0 $9.95

THE EMPIRE STRIKES BACK
George Lucas • Toshiki Kudo
VOLUME 1
ISBN: 1-56971-390-1 $9.95
VOLUME 2
ISBN: 1-56971-391-X $9.95
VOLUME 3
ISBN: 1-56971-392-8 $9.95
VOLUME 4
ISBN: 1-56971-393-6 $9.95

RETURN OF THE JEDI
George Lucas • Shin-ichi Hiromoto
VOLUME 1
ISBN: 1-56971-394-4 $9.95
VOLUME 2
ISBN: 1-56971-395-2 $9.95
VOLUME 3
ISBN: 1-56971-396-0 $9.95
VOLUME 4
ISBN: 1-56971-397-9 $9.95

EPISODE 1–THE PHANTOM MENACE
George Lucas • Kia Asamiya
VOLUME 1
ISBN: 1-56971-483-5 $9.95
VOLUME 2
ISBN: 1-56971-484-3 $9.95

BOBA FETT

DEATH, LIES, & TREACHERY
Wagner • Kennedy
ISBN: 1-56971-311-1 $12.95

ENEMY OF THE EMPIRE
Wagner • Gibson • Nadeau • Ezquerra
ISBN: 1-56971-407-X $12.95

CRIMSON EMPIRE

CRIMSON EMPIRE
Richardson • Stradley • Gulacy • Russell
ISBN: 1-56971-355-3 $17.95

COUNCIL OF BLOOD
Richardson • Stradley • Gulacy • Emberlin
ISBN: 1-56971-410-X $17.95

DARK EMPIRE

DARK EMPIRE
Veitch • Kennedy
ISBN: 1-56971-073-2 $17.95

DARK EMPIRE II
Veitch • Kennedy
ISBN: 1-56971-119-4 $17.95

EMPIRE'S END
Veitch • Baikie
ISBN: 1-56971-306-5 $5.95

DARK FORCES
Prose novellas, heavily illustrated

SOLDIER FOR THE EMPIRE
Dietz • Williams
hardcover edition
ISBN: 1-56971-155-0 $24.95
paperback edition
ISBN: 1-56971-348-0 $14.95

REBEL AGENT
Dietz • Tucker
hardcover edition
ISBN: 1-56971-156-9 $24.95
paperback edition
ISBN: 1-56971-400-2 $14.95

JEDI KNIGHT
Dietz • Dorman
hardcover edition
ISBN: 1-56971-157-7 $24.95
paperback edition
ISBN: 1-56971-433-9 $14.95

DROIDS

THE KALARBA ADVENTURES
Thorsland • Windham • Gibson
ISBN: 1-56971-064-3 $17.95

REBELLION
Windham • Gibson
ISBN: 1-56971-224-7 $14.95

JABBA THE HUTT

THE ART OF THE DEAL
Woodring • Wetherell • Sheldon
ISBN: 1-56971-310-3 $9.95

JEDI ACADEMY

LEVIATHAN
96-page color paperback
ISBN: 1-56971-456-8 $11.95

MARA JADE

BY THE EMPEROR'S HAND
Zahn • Stackpole • Ezquerra
ISBN: 1-56971-401-0 $15.95

PRELUDE TO REBELLION
Strnad • Winn • Jones
ISBN: 1-56971-448-7 $14.95

SHADOWS OF THE EMPIRE

SHADOWS OF THE EMPIRE
Wagner • Plunkett • Russell
ISBN: 1-56971-183-6 $17.95

EVOLUTION
Perry • Randall • Simmons
ISBN: 1-56971-434-7 $14.95

SPLINTER OF THE MIND'S EYE
Austin • Sprouse
ISBN: 1-56971-223-9 $14.95

TALES OF THE JEDI

KNIGHTS OF THE OLD REPUBLIC
Veitch • Gossett
ISBN: 1-56971-020-1 $14.95

THE FREEDON NADD UPRISING
Veitch • Akins • Rodier
ISBN: 1-56971-307-3 $5.95

DARK LORDS OF THE SITH
Veitch • Anderson • Gossett
ISBN: 1-56971-095-3 $17.95

THE SITH WAR
Anderson • Carrasco, Jr.
ISBN: 1-56971-173-9 $17.95

THE GOLDEN AGE OF THE SITH
Anderson • Carrasco, Jr. • Gossett
ISBN: 1-56971-229-8 $16.95

FALL OF THE SITH EMPIRE
Anderson • Heike • Carrasco, Jr.
ISBN: 1-56971-320-0 $14 .95

UNION
Stackpole • Teranishi • Chuckry
ISBN: 1-56971-464-9 $12.95

VADER'S QUEST
Macan • Gibbons
ISBN: 1-56971-415-0 $11.95

THE THRAWN TRILOGY

HEIR TO THE EMPIRE
Baron • Vatine • Blanchard
ISBN: 1-56971-202-6 $19.95

DARK FORCE RISING
Baron • Dodson • Nowlan
ISBN: 1-56971-269-7 $17.95

THE LAST COMMAND
Baron • Biukovic
ISBN: 1-56971-378-2 $17.95

X-WING ROGUE SQUADRON

THE PHANTOM AFFAIR
Stackpole • Macan • Biukovic
ISBN: 1-56971-251-4 $12.95

BATTLEGROUND: TATOOINE
Stackpole • Strnad • Nadeau • Ensign
ISBN: 1-56971-276-X $12.95

THE WARRIOR PRINCESS
Stackpole • Tolson • Nadeau • Ensign
ISBN: 1-56971-330-8 $12.95

REQUIEM FOR A ROGUE
Stackpole • Strnad • Barr • Erskine
ISBN: 1-56971-331-6 $12.95

IN THE EMPIRE'S SERVICE
Stackpole • Nadeau • Ensign
ISBN: 1-56971-383-9 $12.95

BLOOD AND HONOR
Stackpole • Crespo • Hall • Martin
ISBN: 1-56971-387-1 $12.95

MASQUERADE
Stackpole • Johnson • Martin
ISBN: 1-56971-487-8 $12.95

Available from your local comics shop or bookstore!

To find a comics shop in your area, call 1-888-266-4226
For more information or to order direct:
•On the web: www.darkhorse.com •E-mail: mailorder@darkhorse.com
•Phone: 1-800-862-0052 or (503) 652-9701 Mon.-Sat. 9 A.M. to 5 P.M. Pacific Time